COOKING CLASS
CHICKEN
COOKBOOK

PUBLICATIONS INTERNATIONAL, LTD.

All recipes and photographs that contain specific brand names are copyrighted by those companies and/or associations.

DOLE® is a registered trademark of Dole Food Company, Inc.

PYREX is a registered trademark of Corning Incorporated, Corning NY 14831.

Photography on pages 15, 31 and 79 by Vuksanovich, Chicago.

Front cover photography and all other photography by Sacco Productions Limited, Chicago.

ISBN: 0-7853-0191-7

Pictured on the front cover: Pollo alla Firènze (*page 72*).
Pictured on the inside front cover: Forty-Clove Chicken Filice (*page 42*).
Pictured on the back cover: Garlicky Gilroy Chicken Wings (*page 12*).

The publishers would like to thank the following companies and organizations for the use of their recipes in this publication: American Spice Trade Association; A-OK Cook Off; Borden Kitchens, Borden, Inc.; California Apricot Advisory Board; Delmarva Poultry Industry, Inc.; Dole Food Company, Inc.; The Fresh Garlic Association; The HVR Company; Kraft General Foods, Inc.; Thomas J. Lipton Co.; National Broiler Council; New York Cherry Growers Association; Pace Foods, Inc.; Pollio Dairy Products Corporation.

8 7 6 5 4 3 2 1

Manufactured in U.S.A.

CONTENTS

Larry's Pineapple Hula Salad (*page 20*)

Chicken Breasts Sautéed with Sun-Dried Tomatoes (*page 74*)

Stuffed Chicken with Apple Glaze (*page 92*)

CLASS NOTES

Chicken is highly regarded by cooks for its universal appeal. Economical, versatile and readily available, chicken is the perfect ingredient for everyday cooking. Plus, chicken is high in protein and low in fat and cholesterol. Its delicious flavor makes it a winning choice for healthy eating.

The vast selection of chicken products available can make choosing the right ones a challenge. Knowing the differences between types of chicken can help you make the most of this popular ingredient.

CHICKEN BASICS

Chickens are classified by age and weight. Young chickens are tender and cook quickly; older chickens need slow cooking to make them tender. For best results, it's important to know which type of chicken to buy.

Broiler-fryers are young chickens weighing from 1½ to 3½ pounds. Only 7 to 10 weeks old, they yield tender, mildly flavored meat and are best when broiled, fried or roasted.

Roasters are 4- to 6-pound chickens that are 16 weeks old. As the name implies, they are perfect for roasting and rotisserie cooking.

Capons are young, castrated roosters that weigh from 5 to 7 pounds. These richly flavored birds have a higher fat content and yield more meat than roasters.

Stewing hens are adult chickens from 1 to 1½ years old. They weigh from 4½ to 7 pounds and have tough, stringy meat.

Stewing hens are excellent for stocks, soups or stews, since moist-heat preparation tenderizes them and enhances their chicken-y flavor.

Supermarkets fulfill a constant demand for chicken with a variety of chicken cuts and products. Here are some of the more popular choices:

Whole chickens of every type are available with the neck and giblets wrapped separately and stuffed inside. Look for **livers** and **giblets** packaged separately for use in stuffings, soups and specialty dishes.

Cut-up chickens, usually broiler-fryers, are disjointed whole chickens consisting of two breast halves, two thighs, two wings and two drumsticks. Small broiler-fryers are also available in **halves** and **quarters.**

Chicken pieces are available to suit many needs. **Chicken legs** are whole broiler-fryer legs with thighs and drumsticks attached. **Thighs** and **drumsticks** are also packaged separately.

Packaged **chicken wings** are a popular choice for appetizer recipes. **Drumettes** are disjointed wing sections.

Chicken breasts are popular because of their tender, meaty, sweet character. They are available whole or split into halves. (*Note:* One *whole* breast is comprised of two *half* breasts. Recipes in this book that call for *one whole breast* require *both* breast halves.)

Boneless skinless chicken has become a favorite choice for today's busy cook because of its convenience and quick-

cooking appeal. Boneless breasts, also called **cutlets** or **supremes,** plus **chicken tenders** and boneless thighs are some of the cuts of boneless chicken available.

Ground chicken is a recent addition to the poultry case; its most popular use is as a low-fat replacement for ground beef or pork. Processed chicken includes **canned chunk chicken,** newly introduced chicken **sausage,** chicken **franks** and traditional **deli** and **luncheon meats.**

SHOPPING TIPS

Once you have determined the kind of chicken you wish to buy, check out these important tips on inspecting and purchasing chicken.

• Check the package for the U.S.D.A. Grade A rating; chicken in most supermarkets should be government inspected. Look for secure, unbroken packaging, as well as a "sell-by" date stamp that indicates the last day the chicken should be sold.

• Physically inspect the chicken before purchasing. Its skin should be creamy white to deep yellow; meat should never look gray or pasty. Odors could signal spoilage. If you notice a strong, unpleasant odor after opening a package of chicken, leave it open on the counter for a few minutes. Sometimes oxidation takes place inside the package, resulting in a slight, but harmless odor. If the odor remains, return the chicken in its original package to the store for a refund.

• The key to purchasing chicken is knowing what you plan to use it for and then buying according to your needs. After all, chicken is both economical and convenient. If you purchase whole chickens on sale and cut them apart at home, you can save money (see Helpful Preparation Techniques, pages 7–11). Save time by stocking the freezer with ready-to-use boneless skinless chicken. Store the chicken in efficient, meal-size portions; they defrost and cook quickly and eliminate leftovers.

• To make sure you buy enough chicken to meet your family's needs, follow this guide: One broiler-fryer (2 to 3 pounds), cut up, yields 3 to 5 servings; one roaster (3 to 6 pounds) yields 4 to 8 servings. One whole chicken breast or two chicken breast halves (about 12 ounces total) yields 2 servings; one pound of chicken thighs or drumsticks yields about 2 servings.

• As a rule, two whole chicken breasts (about 12 ounces each) yield about 2 cups chopped cooked chicken; one broiler-fryer (about 3 pounds) yields about 2½ cups chopped cooked chicken.

PROPER CHICKEN STORAGE

Fresh, raw chicken can be stored in its original wrap for up to two days in the coldest part of the refrigerator. However, freeze chicken immediately if you do not plan to use it within two days after purchasing. You can freeze most chicken in its original packaging safely for up to two months; if you plan to freeze it longer, consider double-wrapping or rewrapping with freezer paper, aluminum foil or plastic wrap. Airtight packaging is the key to freezing chicken successfully.

When freezing whole chickens, remove and rinse giblets (if any) and pat dry with paper towels. Trim away any excess fat from chicken. Tightly wrap, label, date and freeze both chicken and giblets in separate freezer-strength plastic, paper or foil wraps.

Thaw frozen chicken, wrapped, in the refrigerator for best results. Thawing times for frozen chicken vary depending on how thoroughly frozen the chicken is and whether the chicken is whole or cut up. A general guideline is to allow 24 hours thawing time for a 5-pound whole chicken; allow about 5 hours per pound for thawing chicken pieces. Never thaw chicken on the kitchen counter; this promotes bacterial growth.

A WORD ABOUT HANDLING CHICKEN

When handling raw chicken, you must keep everything that comes into contact with it clean. Raw chicken should be rinsed and patted dry with paper towels before cooking; cutting boards and knives must be washed in hot sudsy water after using and hands must be scrubbed thoroughly before and after handling. Why? Raw chicken can harbor harmful salmonella bacteria. If bacteria are transferred to work surfaces, utensils or hands, they could contaminate other foods as well as the cooked chicken and cause food poisoning. With careful handling and proper cooking, this is easily prevented.

Chicken should always be cooked completely before eating. You should never cook chicken partially, then store it to be finished later, since this promotes bacterial growth as well.

IS IT DONE YET?

There are a number of ways to determine if chicken is thoroughly cooked and ready to eat. For whole chickens, a meat thermometer inserted into the thickest part of the thigh, but not near bone or fat, should register 180° to 185°F before removing from the oven. If a whole chicken is stuffed, insert the thermometer into the center of the body cavity; when the stuffing registers 160°F, the chicken should be done. (*Note:* Chicken should only be stuffed *just before* roasting; *never* stuff a chicken ahead of time.) Roasted whole chicken breasts are done when they register 170°F on a meat thermometer.

To test bone-in chicken pieces, you should be able to insert a fork into the chicken with ease and the juices should run clear; however, the meat and juices nearest the bones might still be a little pink even though the chicken is cooked thoroughly. Boneless chicken pieces are done when the centers are no longer pink; you can determine this by simply cutting into the chicken with a knife.

HELPFUL PREPARATION TECHNIQUES

Flattening uncooked boneless chicken breasts

Place one chicken breast half between two sheets of waxed paper. Using flat side of meat mallet or rolling pin, gently pound chicken from center to outside of chicken to desired thickness.

Skinning uncooked chicken

Freeze chicken until firm, but not hard. (However, do not refreeze thawed chicken.) Grasp skin with clean cotton kitchen towel and pull away from meat; discard skin. When finished skinning chicken, launder towel before using again.

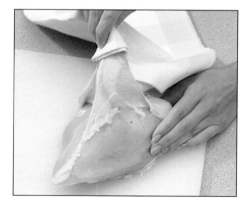

Disjointing a Whole Chicken

1. Place chicken, breast side up, on cutting board. Cut between thigh and body to hip joint. Bend leg back slightly to free hip

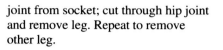

joint from socket; cut through hip joint and remove leg. Repeat to remove other leg.

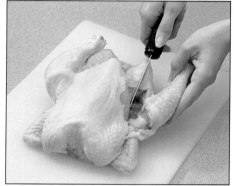

2. Place leg, skin side down, on cutting board. Locate joint by moving thigh back and forth with one hand while holding drumstick with other hand. Cut completely through joint.

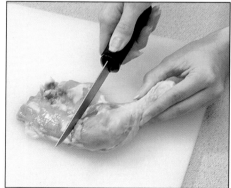

3. Place chicken on side. Pull one wing out from body; cut through shoulder joint. Turn chicken over and repeat to remove other wing.

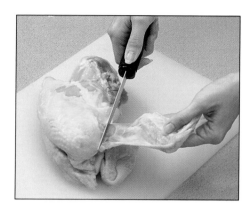

4. Working from tail to neck, cut breast from backbone, cutting through small rib bones and along outside of collarbone.

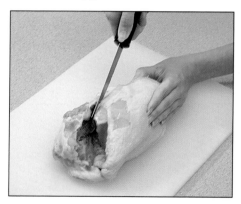

5. Turn chicken over and repeat on other side. Cut through any remaining connective tissue; pull breast away from backbone.

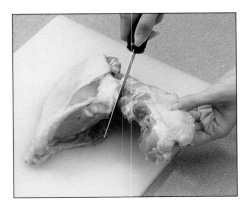

6. Place breast, skin side up, on cutting board. Split breast into halves by cutting along one side of breastbone. If desired, you may debone the whole breast before splitting (see Skinning and Deboning a Whole Chicken Breast, pages 10–11, steps 1–8).

Cutting a Whole Chicken into Halves and Quarters

1. Place chicken, breast side down, on cutting board with neck end away from you. Working from neck to tail, cut along one side of backbone, cutting as close to bone as possible. Cut down other side of backbone; remove backbone.

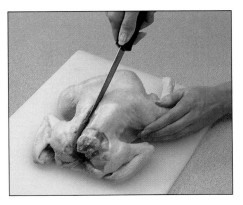

2. Remove breastbone (see Skinning and Deboning a Whole Chicken Breast, pages 7–8, steps 2–7).

3. Turn chicken, skin side up. Cut lengthwise down center of chicken to split into halves.

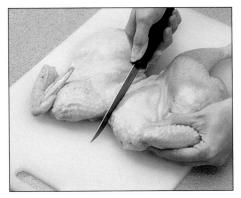

4. To cut into quarters, cut through skin separating thighs from breast.

Skinning and Deboning a Whole Chicken Breast

1. Freeze chicken breast until firm, but not hard. (However, do not refreeze thawed chicken.) Grasp skin with clean cotton kitchen towel and pull away from meat; discard skin. When finished skinning chicken breast, launder towel before using again.

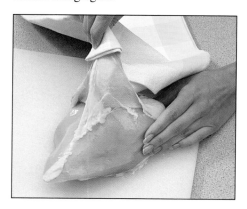

2. Place breast, meaty side down, on cutting board. Cut small slit through membrane and cartilage at the V of the neck end.

3. Grasp breast with both hands and gently bend both sides backward to snap breastbone.

4. With fingers, work along both sides of breastbone to loosen triangular keel bone; pull out bone.

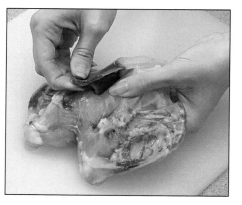

5. With tip of sharp knife, cut along both sides of cartilage at end of breastbone. Remove cartilage.

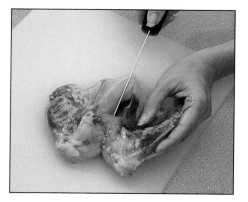

6. Slip point of knife under long rib bone on one side of breast. Cut and scrape meat from rib bones, pulling bones away from meat.

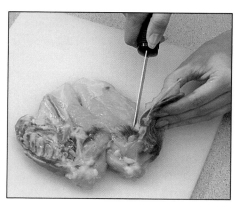

7. Cut meat away from collarbone. Remove bones. Repeat procedure to debone other side of breast.

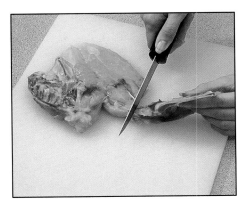

8. Remove wishbones of chicken breasts that have been cut from whole chickens in your home kitchen. Cut meat away from wishbone at neck end of breast. Grasp wishbone and pull it out of breast.

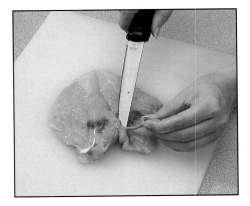

9. To remove white tendon from each side of breast, cut enough meat away from each tendon so you can grasp it (use paper towel for firmer grasp). Remove tendon.

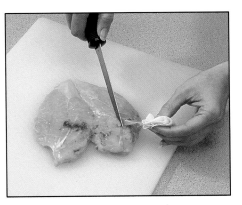

10. Turn breast, meaty side up. If desired, remove chicken tenders from thickest edge of each breast half and reserve for another use. Trim any loosened remaining connective tissue, if needed. Cut whole chicken breast lengthwise into halves, if desired.

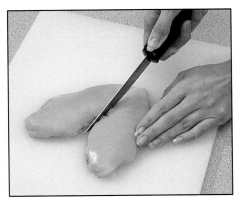

Shredding cooked chicken

Place cooked boneless skinless chicken on cutting board. Pull meat into long shreds with two forks or fingers.

Garlicky Gilroy Chicken Wings

2 **pounds chicken wings
(about 15 wings)**
3 **heads fresh garlic***
Boiling water
1 **cup *plus* 1 tablespoon olive oil,
divided**
10 **to 15 drops Tabasco® brand
pepper sauce**
1 **cup grated Parmesan cheese**
1 **cup Italian-style bread crumbs**
1 **teaspoon black pepper
Carrot and celery slices for
garnish**

*The whole garlic bulb is called a head.

1. Preheat oven to 375°F.

2. Locate first and second joints in chicken wings. Cut through both joints for each wing using sharp knife on cutting board; remove and discard tips. Rinse wing sections; pat dry with paper towels.

3. To peel whole heads of garlic, drop garlic heads into enough boiling water in small saucepan to cover for 5 to 10 seconds. Immediately remove garlic with slotted spoon. Plunge garlic into cold water; drain. Peel away skins.

4. Place garlic, 1 cup oil and Tabasco® sauce in food processor; cover and process until smooth.

5. Pour garlic mixture into small bowl. Combine cheese, bread crumbs and black pepper in shallow dish. Dip wing sections, one at a time, into garlic mixture, then roll in crumb mixture, coating evenly and shaking off excess.

6. Brush 13 × 9-inch nonstick baking pan with remaining 1 tablespoon oil; arrange wing sections in single layer in pan. Drizzle remaining garlic mixture over wing sections; sprinkle with remaining crumb mixture.

7. Bake 45 to 60 minutes or until chicken is brown and crisp. Garnish, if desired.

Makes about 6 servings

Step 2. Cutting chicken wings into sections.

Step 3. Removing blanched garlic from boiling water.

Step 5. Coating chicken wing sections.

Savory Mexican Potato Tart

3 medium russet potatoes (about 1 pound), peeled
Water
½ cup all-purpose flour
¼ cup cornmeal
4 tablespoons vegetable oil, divided
½ teaspoon garlic salt
½ teaspoon black pepper
1 medium onion
1 jar (8 ounces) mild taco sauce
1 cup shredded cooked chicken (page 11)
1 cup (4 ounces) shredded Monterey Jack cheese
1 small jalapeño pepper, seeded and minced
2 tablespoons chopped fresh oregano
Prepared guacamole
Cilantro leaves for garnish

1. Place potatoes in large saucepan; add enough water to cover. Bring to a boil over high heat. Reduce heat to low; cover and simmer 30 minutes or until potatoes are fork-tender. Drain. Mash potatoes in large bowl with hand mixer at low speed.

2. Preheat oven to 350°F.

3. Combine warm mashed potatoes, flour, cornmeal, 3 tablespoons oil, garlic salt and black pepper in large bowl; mix into smooth dough.

4. Dust hands with flour. Press potato mixture into bottom and up side of ungreased 10-inch flan or tart pan with removable bottom; set aside.

5. Chop onion (technique on page 32).

6. Combine taco sauce with onion in small bowl; spread evenly over potato mixture. Top with chicken, cheese and jalapeño. Sprinkle with oregano and remaining 1 tablespoon oil.

7. Bake 30 minutes or until potato mixture is heated through. Cool tart slightly, about 10 minutes.

8. Carefully loosen tart from rim of pan using table knife. Remove rim from pan.

9. Remove potato tart from pan bottom; cut into wedges. Serve with guacamole. Garnish, if desired. *Makes 8 servings*

Step 1. Mashing potatoes.

Step 4. Pressing potato mixture into pan.

Step 8. Loosening tart from rim of pan.

Dipper's Nuggets Chicken

2 whole chicken breasts, split, skinned and boned (pages 10–11)
Vegetable oil
1 egg
⅓ cup water
⅓ cup all-purpose flour
2 teaspoons sesame seed
1½ teaspoons salt
Sweet and sour sauce, cocktail sauce and tartar sauce for dipping
Red onion rings for garnish

1. Cut chicken into 1-inch pieces on cutting board; set aside.

2. Heat 3 inches of oil in large, heavy saucepan over medium-high heat until oil registers 375°F on deep-fry thermometer. Adjust heat to maintain temperature.

3. Meanwhile, beat egg and water in large bowl until blended. Add flour, sesame seed and salt, mixing into smooth batter.

4. Dip chicken pieces into batter, a few at a time, shaking off excess.

5. Fry chicken, a few pieces at a time, in hot oil about 4 minutes or until chicken is golden brown and no longer pink in center. With slotted spoon, remove chicken to paper towels to drain.

6. Serve with sauces. Garnish, if desired.

Makes 8 servings

Step 1. Cutting chicken into 1-inch pieces.

Step 3. Mixing batter.

Step 4. Dipping chicken pieces into batter.

Chicken Pizza

1 package (8 ounces) refrigerated
   crescent rolls
2 whole chicken breasts, split,
   skinned and boned (pages
   10–11)
1 large green bell pepper
1 large onion
¼ cup vegetable oil
½ pound sliced mushrooms
½ cup pitted ripe olives, sliced
1 can (10½ ounces) pizza sauce
   with cheese
1 teaspoon garlic salt
1 teaspoon dried oregano leaves,
   crushed
¼ cup grated Parmesan cheese
2 cups (8 ounces) shredded
   mozzarella cheese

1. Preheat oven to 425°F.

2. Separate dough into eight triangles. Press triangles into greased 12-inch pizza pan, covering bottom of pan completely. Seal seams; set aside.

3. Cut chicken into 1-inch pieces on cutting board; set aside.

4. To prepare bell pepper, with paring knife, make circular cut around top of pepper. Pull stem from pepper to remove stem, seeds and membrane. Rinse out pepper under running water to remove any excess seeds; drain well.

5. Thinly slice pepper crosswise into rings on cutting board; remove any excess membrane.

6. Chop onion (technique on page 32).

7. Heat oil in large skillet over medium-high heat. Add chicken, pepper, onion, mushrooms and olives. Cook and stir 5 minutes or until chicken is no longer pink in center.

8. Spread pizza sauce over dough. Spoon chicken mixture over top. Sprinkle with garlic salt, oregano and Parmesan. Top with mozzarella cheese.

9. Bake 20 minutes or until crust is golden brown. Cut into wedges to serve. Garnish as desired. *Makes 8 servings*

Step 2. Pressing dough triangles into pan.

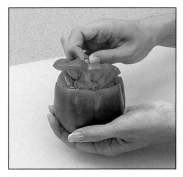

Step 4. Removing stem, seeds and membranes from pepper.

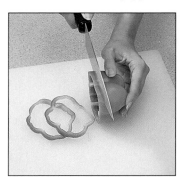

Step 5. Slicing pepper into rings.

Larry's Pineapple Hula Salad

1 papaya
2 whole chicken breasts, split, skinned, boned (pages 10–11) and cooked
1 large rib celery
2 cans (8 ounces *each*) Dole® Pineapple Chunks, drained
½ cup macadamia nuts or peanuts
1 cup mayonnaise
2 teaspoons curry powder
Salad greens
Chives and sliced kumquats for garnish

1. To prepare papaya, slice papaya lengthwise in half on cutting board. With large spoon, scoop out seeds; discard. Remove peel from papaya using vegetable peeler or paring knife.

2. Dice enough papaya to measure 1 cup. Reserve remainder for other use.*

3. Dice chicken on cutting board; set aside.

4. To prepare celery, trim stem end and leaves from celery rib on cutting board. Slice celery diagonally.

5. Combine papaya, chicken, celery, pineapple and nuts in large bowl.

6. Blend mayonnaise and curry in small bowl.

7. Spoon mayonnaise mixture over chicken mixture; blend thoroughly. Cover; refrigerate salad at least 1 hour.

8. Serve salad mounded on salad-green-lined serving platter. Garnish, if desired.

Makes 4 servings

*For best results, store leftover papaya tightly wrapped in the refrigerator. Cut papaya should be eaten within two days.

Step 1. Removing peel from papaya.

Step 2. Dicing papaya.

Step 3. Dicing chicken.

Hot Chinese Chicken Salad

8 boneless skinless chicken thighs
1 large tomato
¼ cup cornstarch
¼ cup vegetable oil
1 can (4 ounces) water chestnuts, drained and sliced
1 can (4 ounces) sliced mushrooms, drained
1 cup coarsely chopped green onions
1 cup diagonally sliced celery
¼ cup soy sauce
⅛ teaspoon garlic powder
2 cups finely shredded iceberg lettuce
  Orange slices for garnish
  Hot cooked rice

1. Cut chicken into bite-size pieces on cutting board; set aside.

2. To prepare tomato, with paring knife, make circular cut around stem end using sawing motion. Remove stem end. Cut tomato in half on cutting board; cut each half into bite-size pieces. Set aside.

3. Place cornstarch in shallow dish.

4. Place chicken, one piece at a time, in cornstarch. Coat evenly, shaking off excess; set aside.

5. Place wok or large skillet over high heat. (Test hot pan by adding drop of water to pan; if water sizzles, pan is sufficiently hot.) Add oil to wok, swirling to coat all sides. Heat oil until hot, about 30 seconds.

6. Add chicken to wok; stir-fry chicken with wok utensil or wooden spoon, keeping chicken in constant motion, 3 minutes or until chicken is no longer pink in center.

7. Stir in tomato, water chestnuts, mushrooms, green onions, celery, soy sauce and garlic powder. Cover; simmer 5 minutes.

8. Place chicken mixture on lettuce-lined serving platter. Garnish, if desired. Serve with rice.
Makes 4 servings

Step 2. Removing stem from tomato.

Step 4. Coating chicken with cornstarch.

Step 6. Stir-frying chicken.

Lagoon Chicken Salad

1½ cups unsweetened apple juice
2 whole chicken breasts
    (about 1½ pounds)
1 medium apple
3 cups cooled cooked rice
    (1 cup uncooked)
1½ cups seedless green grapes,
    halved
½ cup chopped celery
¾ cup slivered almonds, divided
½ cup chopped water chestnuts
1 cup mayonnaise
½ teaspoon seasoned salt
¼ teaspoon ground cinnamon
    Spinach leaves
    Apple slices for garnish

1. To poach chicken, simmer apple juice in deep saucepan over medium heat; add chicken. Cover; simmer about 30 minutes or until chicken is tender. Remove chicken from saucepan to cool; discard liquid.

2. When chicken is cool enough to handle, carefully remove and discard skin and bones.

3. Dice chicken on cutting board. Place in large bowl; set aside.

4. To prepare apple, cut lengthwise into quarters on cutting board; remove stem, core and seeds with paring knife. Chop apple quarters into ½-inch pieces. Toss with chicken in bowl.

5. Gently toss chicken, apple, rice, grapes, celery, ½ cup almonds and water chestnuts; set aside.

6. Combine mayonnaise, seasoned salt and cinnamon in small bowl.

7. Add mayonnaise mixture to chicken mixture; toss lightly. Cover; refrigerate chicken salad at least 30 minutes.

8. Spoon chicken salad onto spinach-lined serving platter. Sprinkle with remaining ¼ cup almonds. Garnish, if desired.

Makes 4 to 6 servings

Step 2. Removing bones from chicken.

Step 3. Dicing chicken.

Step 4. Removing stem, core and seeds from apple.

Chicken and Walnut Salad Athena

½ cup extra virgin olive oil
½ cup lemon juice
1 tablespoon light brown sugar
1 package (1 ounce) Hidden Valley
  Ranch® Salad Dressing Mix
2 cups diced cooked chicken
¼ cup loosely packed fresh
  parsley, minced
1 green onion, thinly sliced
4 ounces fresh feta cheese
  Cold water
2 tablespoons margarine
½ teaspoon dried rosemary
  leaves, crushed
1 cup walnut halves
3 small ripe tomatoes
6 radishes, thinly sliced
12 California ripe olives, sliced
  Crisp salad greens
  Rosemary sprigs and radish
  slices for garnish

1. Combine oil, lemon juice, sugar and salad dressing mix in glass jar with tightly fitting lid. Cover; shake until dressing is well blended.

2. Pour dressing into large bowl. Add chicken, turning to coat with dressing. Stir in parsley and green onion. Cover; marinate in refrigerator at least 1 hour or overnight.

3. Remove feta from package; drain. Place feta in small bowl; cover with cold water and soak 5 minutes to remove excess salt.

4. Meanwhile, melt margarine with ½ teaspoon rosemary in small, heavy skillet over low heat. Add walnuts; cook 5 minutes or until walnuts are lightly toasted, stirring occasionally. Remove skillet from heat; cool walnuts.

5. Remove feta from water; pat dry. Discard water. Using fingers, crumble feta into small chunks. Return feta to bowl; set aside.

6. To prepare tomato, with paring knife, make circular cut around stem end using sawing motion. Remove stem end. Cut each stemmed tomato lengthwise into halves on cutting board; cut each half lengthwise into three or four wedges.

7. To serve, stir feta, walnuts, radishes and olives into chicken mixture; toss until well mixed. Arrange chicken mixture and tomatoes on salad-green-lined plates. Garnish, if desired.   *Makes 6 servings*

Step 4. Toasting walnuts.

Step 5. Crumbling feta.

Step 6. Removing stem from tomato.

Montmorency Cherry Chicken Salad

2 cups tart red Montmorency cherries*
1½ whole chicken breasts, split, skinned, boned (pages 10–11) and cooked
3 nectarines or peaches
Lemon juice
1½ cups sliced celery
2 tablespoons sliced green onion
1 cup mayonnaise
¼ cup sour cream
2 tablespoons honey
¼ to ½ teaspoon curry powder
⅛ teaspoon ground ginger
Salt to taste
½ cup slivered almonds
Boston or Bibb lettuce leaves

*If fresh Montmorency cherries are unavailable, substitute any fresh sour cherry. You may substitute equal amounts of frozen pitted cherries if fresh are unavailable; thaw and drain cherries well and skip step 1.

1. To pit cherries, slice an X into ends of cherries with paring knife; squeeze out cherry pits with thumb and forefinger. Set cherries aside.

2. Dice chicken on cutting board.

3. To prepare one nectarine, insert knife blade into stem end; slice in half lengthwise to the pit, turning nectarine while slicing. Remove knife blade; twist halves to pull apart. Remove pit from nectarine; discard. Cut nectarine halves into ½-inch slices on cutting board; place in large bowl and set aside. Prepare remaining two nectarines in same manner; brush with lemon juice and reserve for garnish.

4. Combine cherries, chicken, celery and green onion in large bowl with nectarine slices. Set aside. Combine mayonnaise, sour cream, honey, 1 teaspoon lemon juice, curry, ginger and salt in small bowl; mix well. Pour mayonnaise mixture over chicken mixture; toss to coat. Cover; refrigerate.

5. To toast almonds, spread on baking sheet. Bake in preheated 350°F oven 8 to 10 minutes or until golden brown; stir frequently. Remove almonds from baking sheet and cool; set aside.

6. Stir all but 1 tablespoon almonds into salad just before serving; arrange salad on lettuce-lined plates. Arrange remaining nectarine slices around salad. Sprinkle salad with remaining 1 tablespoon almonds.

Makes 6 servings

Step 1. Squeezing pit from cherry.

Step 3. Removing pits from nectarines.

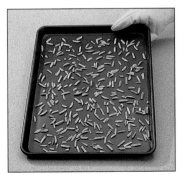

Step 5. Toasted almonds.

Lipton® Fried Rice with Chicken

1 clove garlic
1½ whole chicken breasts, split, skinned and boned (pages 10–11)
Vegetable oil
1 cup chopped bok choy (Chinese white cabbage)
1 cup fresh snow peas, trimmed
¼ cup sliced green onions
1 envelope Lipton® Recipe Secrets Onion-Mushroom Recipe Soup Mix
¾ cup water
1 tablespoon soy sauce
⅛ teaspoon pepper
2 cups hot cooked brown or white rice (cooked in unsalted water) (about ⅔ cup uncooked)

1. To prepare garlic, trim ends of clove on cutting board. Slightly crush garlic under flat side of knife blade; peel away skin.

2. Chop garlic until minced.

3. Cut chicken into strips on cutting board; set aside.

4. Place wok or large skillet over high heat. (Test hot pan by adding drop of water to pan; if water sizzles, pan is sufficiently hot.) Add oil to wok, swirling to coat all sides. Heat oil until hot, about 30 seconds.

5. Add garlic, bok choy, peas and green onions to wok; briskly toss and stir vegetables with wok utensil or wooden spoon, keeping vegetables in constant motion, 3 minutes or until vegetables are crisp-tender. Remove vegetables from wok; set aside.

6. Reheat wok over high heat. Add 2 tablespoons oil to wok, swirling to coat all sides. Heat oil until hot, about 30 seconds.

7. Add chicken to wok; briskly toss and stir chicken with wok utensil or wooden spoon, keeping chicken in constant motion, 3 to 5 minutes or until chicken is no longer pink in center.

8. Thoroughly blend onion-mushroom soup mix, water, soy sauce and pepper in small bowl. Pour soup mixture into wok; toss with chicken to coat.

9. Stir vegetables and cooked rice into chicken in wok until well combined; toss to heat through. To serve, place fried rice on serving platter.
Makes 4 servings

Step 1. Crushing garlic.

Step 2. Minced garlic.

Step 3. Cutting chicken into strips.

Stir-Fried Chicken

1 medium green bell pepper
1 small onion
2 tablespoons soy sauce
2 teaspoons cornstarch
2 whole chicken breasts, split,
   skinned and boned
   (pages 10–11)
   Vegetable oil
1 cup diagonally sliced celery
1 medium carrot, diagonally
   sliced
1 cup sliced mushrooms
1 teaspoon salt
¼ teaspoon ground ginger
1 can (16 ounces) bean sprouts,
   drained
1 can (5 ounces) water chestnuts,
   drained, sliced
¼ cup water
3 cups hot cooked rice
   (1 cup uncooked)
¾ cup peanuts
   Celery leaves for garnish

1. To prepare bell pepper, with paring knife, make circular cut around top of pepper. Pull stem from pepper to remove stem, seeds and membrane.

2. Rinse out pepper under running water to remove any excess seeds; drain well. Slice pepper lengthwise in half on cutting board; remove any excess membrane. Thinly slice each half lengthwise into thin strips.

3. To prepare onion, peel skin from onion; cut in half through the root. Reserve one half for another use. Place other half, cut side down, on cutting board. To coarsely chop onion, hold knife horizontally. Make cuts parallel to board, almost to root end. Next, make vertical, lengthwise cuts, then slice across cuts to root end. (The closer the cuts are spaced, the finer the onion is chopped.)

4. Blend soy sauce into cornstarch in cup until smooth; set aside.

5. Slice chicken across the grain into ¼-inch strips on cutting board.

6. Place wok or large skillet over high heat. (Test hot pan by adding drop of water to pan; if water sizzles, pan is sufficiently hot.) Add 2 tablespoons oil to wok, swirling to coat all sides. Heat oil until hot, about 30 seconds.

continued on page 34

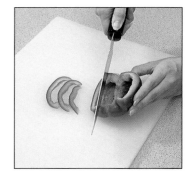

Step 2. Slicing pepper into thin strips.

Step 3. Chopping onion.

Step 5. Cutting chicken into thin strips.

Stir-Fried Chicken, continued

7. Add chicken to wok; stir-fry chicken with wok utensil or wooden spoon, keeping chicken in constant motion, 3 to 5 minutes or until chicken is no longer pink in center. Remove chicken from wok; set aside.

8. Reheat wok over high heat. Add 1 tablespoon oil to wok, swirling to coat all sides. Heat oil until hot, about 30 seconds.

9. Add bell pepper, onion, celery, carrot, mushrooms, salt and ginger to wok; briskly toss and stir vegetables with wok utensil or wooden spoon, keeping vegetables in constant motion, 9 minutes or until vegetables are crisp-tender, adding more oil to wok if needed.

10. Stir chicken into vegetables in wok until well combined; stir in bean sprouts, water chestnuts and water.

11. Push chicken-vegetable mixture to side of wok. Stir soy sauce mixture; stir into wok. Cook and stir until mixture comes to a boil and thickens.

12. Mound rice onto serving platter; spoon chicken-vegetable mixture over rice. Sprinkle with peanuts. Garnish, if desired.   *Makes 6 servings*

Step 7. Stir-frying chicken.

Step 11. Cooking cornstarch mixture.

Chicken Cherry-Yaki Stir-Fry

1 small piece fresh ginger, ¾ inch long
2 whole chicken breasts, split, skinned and boned (pages 10–11)
2 tablespoons teriyaki sauce
2 tablespoons dry sherry
1 tablespoon lemon juice
4 green onions for garnish
  Cold water
6 to 8 ice cubes
¼ cup slivered almonds
1½ cups tart red cherries, pitted (frozen or canned)
2 ounces Chinese rice stick noodles
  Peanut or vegetable oil
1 tablespoon cornstarch
6 green onions, diagonally sliced into 1-inch pieces
2 small carrots, thinly sliced
2 cups snow peas
4 ounces sliced water chestnuts, drained

1. To prepare fresh ginger, peel tough skin from ginger with paring knife or vegetable peeler. Cut ginger into three equal pieces; set aside.

2. Cut chicken into bite-size pieces on cutting board; set aside.

3. Combine ginger pieces, teriyaki sauce, sherry and lemon juice in medium bowl. Add chicken, turning to coat with marinade. Cover; marinate in refrigerator 1 hour.

4. Meanwhile, to prepare green onion brushes for garnish, trim off stems (green part) of 4 onions to make 4-inch lengths.

5. Using sharp scissors, cut each onion lengthwise into very thin strips, leaving one end uncut. Fill large bowl about half full with cold water. Add prepared green onions and ice cubes. Refrigerate until onions curl, about 1 hour; drain.

6. To toast almonds, spread almonds on baking sheet. Bake in preheated 350°F oven 8 to 10 minutes or until golden brown; stir frequently. Remove almonds from baking sheet and cool; set aside.

7. Thaw cherries, if frozen, in medium bowl. Drain cherries, reserving juice; set aside.

continued on page 36

Step 4. Trimming green onions to make 4-inch lengths.

Step 5. Cutting ends of green onions lengthwise.

Step 6. Toasted almonds.

Chicken Cherry-Yaki Stir-Fry,
continued

8. To prepare rice stick noodles, cut noodle bundles in half; gently pull each half apart into smaller bunches. Heat 3 inches oil in wok or large skillet over medium-high heat until deep-fry thermometer registers 375°F. Using tongs or slotted spoon, lower 1 bunch of noodles into hot oil.

9. Cook until noodles rise to the top, 3 to 5 seconds. Remove noodles immediately to paper towels using slotted spoon; drain. Repeat with remaining bunches. Keep noodles warm until ready to serve. Drain; discard oil.

10. Drain chicken, reserving marinade. Discard ginger pieces. Blend reserved cherry juice into cornstarch in cup until smooth. Stir in reserved marinade; set aside.

11. Reheat wok over high heat. Add 2 tablespoons oil to wok, swirling to coat all sides. Heat oil until hot, about 30 seconds. Add chicken to wok; briskly toss and stir chicken with wok utensil or wooden spoon, keeping chicken in constant motion, 2 to 3 minutes or until chicken is no longer pink in center. Remove chicken from wok; set aside.

12. Reheat wok over high heat. Add 2 tablespoons oil to wok, swirling to coat all sides. Heat oil until hot, about 30 seconds.

13. Add sliced green onions, carrots and snow peas to wok; briskly toss and stir vegetables with wok utensil or wooden spoon, keeping vegetables in constant motion, 2 to 3 minutes or until vegetables are crisp-tender, adding more oil to wok if needed.

14. Stir chicken into vegetables in wok until well combined. Push chicken-vegetable mixture to side of wok. Stir cornstarch mixture; stir into wok. Cook and stir until mixture comes to a boil and thickens. Stir in cherries and water chestnuts; heat through.

15. Serve chicken-vegetable mixture over rice stick noodles. Sprinkle with almonds. Garnish with green onion brushes.   *Makes 4 servings*

Step 8. Lowering noodles into hot oil.

Step 9. Cooked noodles.

Apple Curry Chicken

2 whole chicken breasts, split, skinned and boned (pages 10–11)
1 cup apple juice, divided
1/4 teaspoon salt
Dash of pepper
1 medium apple
1 medium onion
1 1/2 cups plain croutons
1/4 cup raisins
2 teaspoons brown sugar
1 teaspoon curry powder
3/4 teaspoon poultry seasoning
1/8 teaspoon garlic powder
2 apple slices and fresh thyme sprigs for garnish

1. Preheat oven to 350°F. Lightly grease 1-quart round baking dish.

2. Arrange chicken breasts in single layer in prepared dish.

3. Combine 1/4 cup apple juice, salt and pepper in small bowl. Brush all of juice mixture over chicken.

4. To prepare apple, cut lengthwise into quarters on cutting board; remove stem, core and seeds with paring knife. Chop apple quarters into 1/2-inch pieces; place in large bowl.

5. To prepare onion, peel skin from onion; cut in half through the root. Place, cut side down, on cutting board. To coarsely chop onion, hold knife horizontally. Make cuts parallel to board, almost to root end. Next, make vertical, lengthwise cuts, then slice across cuts to root end. (The closer the cuts are spaced, the finer the onion is chopped.) Toss chopped onion with apples in bowl.

6. Stir croutons, raisins, brown sugar, curry, poultry seasoning and garlic powder into apple-onion mixture. Toss with remaining 3/4 cup apple juice.

7. Spread crouton mixture over chicken.

8. Cover with foil or lid; bake 45 minutes or until chicken is tender. Garnish, if desired.

Makes 4 servings

Step 3. Brushing chicken with juice mixture.

Step 4. Removing stem, core and seeds from apple.

Step 7. Spreading crouton mixture over chicken.

Chicken Mexicana

2 whole chicken breasts, split,
  skinned and boned
  (pages 10–11)
1/4 teaspoon garlic salt
1 small green bell pepper
2 tablespoons butter
1/2 cup sliced green onions with
  tops (1/2-inch slices)
2 to 3 cups hot cooked rice
  (2/3 to 1 cup uncooked)
4 ounces pasteurized process
  cheese spread
1 cup Pace® picante sauce
  Additional Pace® picante sauce
  Green onion strips for garnish

1. Sprinkle chicken with garlic salt; set aside.

2. Prepare bell pepper for chopping (technique on page 32). Chop bell pepper.

3. Melt butter in large skillet over medium heat until foamy. Add chicken to skillet in single layer. Cook 5 minutes. Turn chicken over; add bell pepper and green onions around edge of skillet. Cook 5 minutes or until chicken is tender and no longer pink in center.

4. Place rice on serving platter. Remove chicken and vegetables from skillet; reserve drippings. Arrange chicken and vegetables over rice; keep warm.

5. To cube process cheese spread, slice cheese into 1/2-inch-thick slices on cutting board.

6. Stack slices; cut slices into 1/2-inch sticks. Holding sticks together in original stack, cut sticks crosswise into cubes.

7. Add cubed process cheese spread and 1 cup picante sauce to reserved drippings in skillet. Cook and stir until cheese is melted and sauce is hot.

8. Pour sauce over chicken and vegetables. Serve with additional picante sauce. Garnish, if desired. *Makes 4 servings*

Step 2. Chopped bell pepper.

Step 5. Slicing process cheese spread.

Step 6. Cubed process cheese spread.

Forty-Clove Chicken Filice

1 (3-pound) frying chicken, cut into serving pieces (page 8–9)
40 cloves garlic (about 2 heads*)
1 lemon
½ cup dry white wine
¼ cup dry vermouth
¼ cup olive oil
4 ribs celery, thickly sliced
2 tablespoons finely chopped parsley
2 teaspoons dried basil leaves, crushed
1 teaspoon dried oregano leaves, crushed
   Pinch of crushed red pepper flakes
   Salt and black pepper to taste

*The whole garlic bulb is called a head.

1. Preheat oven to 375°F. Place chicken, skin side up, in single layer in shallow baking pan; set aside.

2. Peel whole heads of garlic (technique on page 12); set aside.

3. To prepare lemon, hold lemon in one hand. With other hand, remove colored portion of peel with vegetable peeler or zester into small bowl.

4. To juice lemon, cut lemon in half on cutting board; with tip of knife, remove visible seeds.

5. Using citrus reamer or squeezing tightly with hand, squeeze juice from lemon into small glass or dish; remove any remaining seeds from juice.

6. Combine garlic, wine, vermouth, oil, celery, parsley, basil, oregano and red pepper flakes in medium bowl; mix thoroughly. Sprinkle garlic mixture over chicken. Place zest over and around chicken in pan; pour lemon juice over top of chicken. Season with salt and black pepper.

7. Cover pan with foil. Bake 40 minutes.

8. Remove foil; bake 15 minutes or until chicken is tender and juices run clear. Garnish as desired. *Makes 4 to 6 servings*

Step 3. Removing peel from lemon.

Step 4. Removing seeds from lemon.

Step 5. Squeezing juice from lemon.

Olympic Seoul Chicken

2 tablespoons peanut oil
8 chicken thighs, skinned
(page 8)
10 cloves garlic
¼ cup white vinegar
3 tablespoons soy sauce
2 tablespoons honey
¼ teaspoon ground ginger
½ to 1 teaspoon crushed red
pepper flakes
2 ounces Chinese rice stick
noodles
Snow peas, steamed
Diagonally sliced yellow
squash, steamed

1. Heat oil in large skillet over medium-high heat. Add chicken to skillet in single layer. Cook 10 minutes or until chicken is evenly browned and no longer pink in center, turning once.

2. Meanwhile, to prepare garlic, trim ends of cloves on cutting board. Slightly crush garlic under flat side of knife blade; peel away skins.

3. Arrange garlic together in small pile; chop coarsely.

4. Combine vinegar, soy sauce, honey and ginger in small bowl; set aside.

5. When chicken is browned, add garlic and red pepper flakes to skillet; cook and stir 2 to 3 minutes.

6. Spoon off excess fat from skillet. Add vinegar mixture. Cover; reduce heat and simmer 15 minutes or until chicken is tender and juices run clear.

7. Meanwhile, prepare rice stick noodles (technique on page 36); keep warm.

8. Uncover skillet; cook 2 minutes or until sauce is reduced and thickened. Place chicken on individual serving plates; spoon sauce over chicken. Serve with rice stick noodles, peas and squash. Garnish as desired.

Makes 4 servings

Step 2. Crushing garlic.

Step 3. Chopped garlic.

Step 7. Lowering noodles into hot oil.

Chicken Picante

1 medium lime
½ cup medium-hot chunky taco
   sauce
¼ cup Dijon-style mustard
3 whole chicken breasts, split,
   skinned and boned
   (pages 10–11)
2 tablespoons butter
   Plain yogurt
   Chopped fresh cilantro and
   lime slices for garnish

1. To juice lime, cut lime in half on cutting board; with tip of knife, remove any visible seeds.

2. Using citrus reamer or squeezing tightly with hand, squeeze juice from lime into small glass or dish; remove any remaining seeds from juice.

3. Combine lime juice, taco sauce and mustard in large bowl. Add chicken, turning to coat with marinade. Cover; marinate in refrigerator at least 30 minutes.

4. Melt butter in large skillet over medium heat until foamy.

5. Drain chicken, reserving marinade. Add chicken to skillet in single layer. Cook 10 minutes or until chicken is lightly browned on both sides.

6. Add reserved marinade to skillet; cook 5 minutes or until chicken is tender and glazed with marinade.

7. Remove chicken to serving platter; keep warm.

8. Boil marinade in skillet over high heat 1 minute; pour over chicken. Serve with yogurt. Garnish, if desired. *Makes 6 servings*

Step 1. Removing seeds from lime.

Step 2. Squeezing juice from lime.

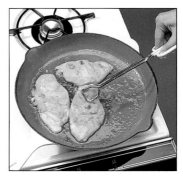
Step 5. Browning chicken.

Chicken with Lime Butter

3 whole chicken breasts, split, skinned and boned (pages 10–11)
¹/₂ teaspoon salt
¹/₂ teaspoon pepper
¹/₃ cup vegetable oil
1 lime
¹/₂ cup butter, softened
1 teaspoon minced fresh chives
¹/₂ teaspoon dried dill weed, crushed
Lime slices, quartered cherry tomatoes and dill sprigs for garnish

1. Sprinkle chicken with salt and pepper.

2. Heat oil in large skillet over medium heat. Add chicken to skillet in single layer. Cook 6 minutes or until chicken is light brown, turning once. Cover; reduce heat to low. Cook 10 minutes or until chicken is tender and no longer pink in center. Remove chicken to serving platter; keep warm.

3. Drain oil from skillet.

4. To juice lime, cut lime in half on cutting board; with tip of knife, remove any visible seeds.

5. Using citrus reamer or squeezing tightly with hand, squeeze juice from lime into skillet; remove any remaining seeds from skillet.

6. Simmer lime juice over low heat 1 minute or until juice begins to bubble.

7. Stir in butter, 1 tablespoon at a time, until sauce thickens.

8. Remove sauce from heat; stir in chives and dill weed.

9. Spoon sauce over chicken. Garnish, if desired.   *Makes 6 servings*

Step 4. Removing seeds from lime.

Step 5. Squeezing juice from lime.

Step 7. Making lime-butter sauce.

Rick's Good-As-Gold Chili

½ cup vegetable oil
2 whole chicken breasts, split, skinned and boned (pages 10–11)
⅓ cup water
¼ cup instant minced onion
2 teaspoons instant minced garlic
1 can (15 ounces) tomato sauce
¾ cup beer
½ cup chicken broth
2 tablespoons chili powder
2 teaspoons ground cumin
1 teaspoon dried oregano leaves, crushed
1 teaspoon soy sauce
1 teaspoon Worcestershire sauce
¾ teaspoon salt
½ teaspoon paprika
½ teaspoon ground red pepper
¼ teaspoon turmeric
⅛ teaspoon rubbed sage
⅛ teaspoon dried thyme leaves, crushed
⅛ teaspoon dry mustard
Jalapeño pepper slices for garnish

1. Heat oil in large skillet over medium-high heat. Add chicken to skillet in single layer. Cook 10 minutes or until chicken is golden brown and no longer pink in center, turning once.

2. Meanwhile, to soften instant onion and garlic, stir together water, onion and garlic in small bowl; let stand 10 minutes.

3. When chicken is browned, remove from skillet and drain on paper towels.

4. When chicken cools slightly, cut into ¼-inch cubes on cutting board; set aside.

5. Drain drippings from skillet, reserving 2 tablespoons. Heat reserved drippings in skillet over medium-high heat. Add softened instant onion and garlic; cook and stir 5 minutes or until onion and garlic are golden.

6. Add cubed chicken and remaining ingredients except jalapeños; stir well. Bring chili to a boil; reduce heat and simmer 20 minutes, stirring occasionally, until chili thickens slightly. Garnish, if desired.

Makes 4½ cups

Step 2. Soften instant onion and garlic.

Step 5. Reserving 2 tablespoons drippings.

Fresh Gazpacho Chicken

¼ cup all-purpose flour
1½ teaspoons salt, divided
½ teaspoon paprika
¼ teaspoon black pepper, divided
2 whole chicken breasts, split
¼ cup vegetable oil
1 medium tomato, seeded and chopped
1 medium onion, chopped (page 32)
1 medium green bell pepper, chopped (page 40)
1 small cucumber
2 cloves garlic, minced (page 30)
2½ cups tomato juice
½ cup finely chopped carrots
½ cup finely chopped celery
½ cup red wine vinegar
¼ cup olive oil
5 teaspoons Worcestershire sauce
5 dashes hot pepper sauce
Hot cooked rice

1. Combine flour, 1 teaspoon salt, paprika and ⅛ teaspoon black pepper in shallow dish. Coat chicken, one piece at a time, in flour mixture, shaking off excess.

2. Heat vegetable oil in large skillet over medium heat; add chicken to skillet in single layer. Cook 10 minutes or until chicken is lightly browned on both sides.

3. Remove chicken to paper-towel-lined baking sheets, using tongs or slotted spoon; keep warm in preheated 200°F oven.

4. Drain oil from skillet.

5. Place tomato, onion and bell pepper in large bowl; set aside.

6. To prepare cucumber, carefully peel skin from cucumber with paring knife. Cut peeled cucumber in half lengthwise on cutting board; remove seeds. Chop cucumber; place in bowl with prepared vegetables and set aside.

7. Stir garlic, tomato juice, carrots, celery, vinegar, olive oil, Worcestershire sauce, pepper sauce, remaining ½ teaspoon salt and remaining ⅛ teaspoon black pepper into large bowl with prepared vegetables.

8. Reserve 1 cup tomato mixture; cover and refrigerate.

9. Return chicken to skillet. Pour remaining tomato mixture over chicken. Cover; cook over medium heat, turning chicken occasionally, 30 minutes or until tender.

10. Arrange chicken on serving platter; spoon sauce over chicken. Serve with chilled tomato mixture and rice. Garnish, if desired.

Makes 4 servings

Step 3. Transferring chicken to prepared baking sheets.

Step 6. Peeling cucumber.

Chicken Avocado Boats

3 large ripe avocados
6 tablespoons lemon juice
¾ cup mayonnaise
1½ tablespoons grated onion
¼ teaspoon celery salt
¼ teaspoon garlic powder
  Salt and pepper to taste
2 cups diced cooked chicken
½ cup (2 ounces) shredded sharp
  Cheddar cheese
  Snipped chives for garnish

1. To prepare avocados, on cutting board, insert knife into stem end of each avocado; slice in half lengthwise to the pit, turning avocado while slicing.

2. Remove knife blade; twist both halves to pull apart.

3. Press knife blade into pit; twist knife to pull pit from avocado. Sprinkle each avocado half with 1 tablespoon lemon juice; set aside.

4. Preheat oven to 350°F.

5. Combine mayonnaise, onion, celery salt, garlic powder, salt and pepper in medium bowl. Stir in chicken; mix well.

6. Drain any excess lemon juice from avocado halves.

7. Fill avocado halves with chicken mixture; sprinkle with cheese.

8. Arrange filled avocado halves in single layer in baking dish. Pour water into same dish to depth of ½ inch.

9. Bake filled avocado halves 15 minutes or until cheese melts. Garnish, if desired.

Makes 6 servings

Step 1. Slicing avocado in half.

Step 2. Twisting avocado halves apart.

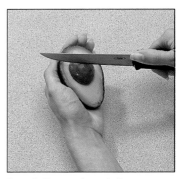
Step 3. Removing pit from avocado.

Calorie-Wise Dill Chicken

Nonstick cooking spray
1 cup plain yogurt
½ cup almonds
1½ cups natural wheat germ
2 teaspoons dried dill weed, crushed
½ teaspoon salt
¼ teaspoon pepper
12 chicken drumsticks

1. Preheat oven to 350°F.

2. Line baking sheet with foil; spray foil with nonstick cooking spray. Set aside.

3. Place yogurt in shallow bowl.

4. Process almonds, about ¼ at a time, with on/off pulses in an electric spice grinder or food process until almost all the almonds are a fine powder. Place ground almonds on shallow plate.

5. Combine wheat germ, almonds, dill weed, salt and pepper in another shallow bowl.

6. Coat drumsticks, one at a time, in yogurt, shaking off excess.

7. Coat drumsticks in wheat germ mixture, shaking off excess.

8. Arrange chicken in single layer on prepared baking sheet.

9. Bake 50 minutes or until chicken is tender and juices run clear. Garnish as desired.

Makes 4 servings

Step 2. Preparing baking sheet.

Step 6. Coating drumsticks in yogurt.

Step 7. Coating drumsticks in wheat germ mixture.

Bittersweet Farm Chicken

½ cup all-purpose flour
1 teaspoon salt
¼ teaspoon pepper
1 (3½- to 4-pound) frying
   chicken, cut into serving
   pieces (pages 8–9)
8 tablespoons butter or
   margarine, divided
1 orange
¼ cup lemon juice
¼ cup orange-flavored liqueur
¼ cup honey
1 tablespoon soy sauce
   Whole cooked baby carrots
   Kumquat slices and lettuce
   leaves for garnish

1. Preheat oven to 350°F.

2. Combine flour, salt and pepper in large resealable plastic bag.

3. Add chicken to bag; shake to coat completely with flour mixture, shaking off excess.

4. Melt 4 tablespoons butter in large baking pan in oven.

5. Remove pan from oven; roll chicken in butter to evenly coat. Arrange chicken, skin side down, in single layer in pan. Bake chicken 30 minutes.

6. Meanwhile, melt remaining 4 tablespoons butter in small saucepan over medium heat.

7. To prepare orange, hold orange in one hand. With other hand, remove colored portion of peel with zester or vegetable peeler into small bowl.

8. Stir orange zest, lemon juice, liqueur, honey and soy sauce into melted butter in saucepan; reserve 2 tablespoons honey mixture.

9. Remove chicken from oven; turn pieces over with tongs.

10. Pour remaining honey mixture over chicken. Continue baking, basting occasionally with pan drippings, 30 minutes or until chicken is glazed and tender.

11. Toss reserved 2 tablespoons honey mixture with desired amount of carrots; serve with chicken. Garnish, if desired.

Makes 4 servings

Step 5. Rolling chicken in melted butter.

Step 7. Removing peel from orange.

Step 9. Turning chicken.

Laguna Beach Pecan Chicken Breasts

6 tablespoons unsalted butter
¼ cup *plus* 2 tablespoons Dijon-style mustard, divided
2 cups pecan halves
4 whole chicken breasts, split, skinned and boned (pages 10–11)
Pepper to taste
1½ to 2 cups plain yogurt
1 cup California sliced pitted ripe olives
1 package (1 ounce) Hidden Valley Ranch® Original Ranch® Salad Dressing Mix
Fresh green beans and pattypan squash, steamed
Mint sprig for garnish

1. Preheat oven to 400°F.

2. Melt butter in small saucepan over low heat; remove from heat.

3. Whisk in ¼ cup mustard; set aside.

4. To grind pecans, process pecan halves in small batches with on/off pulses in food processor to fine powder. Place ground pecans in shallow dish; set aside.

5. Flatten chicken breasts to ¼-inch thickness (technique on pages 7–8). Sprinkle chicken with pepper.

6. Dip chicken into mustard mixture, then roll in ground pecans to coat, shaking off excess.

7. Arrange chicken in single layer in lightly greased baking pan. Bake 15 minutes or until chicken is golden and tender.

8. Meanwhile, thoroughly combine yogurt, olives, salad dressing mix and remaining 2 tablespoons mustard in medium saucepan; set aside.

9. When chicken is done, remove from pan and set aside. Stir drippings from pan into yogurt mixture in saucepan. Simmer mixture over low heat 2 minutes.

10. Place 2 tablespoons yogurt sauce on each serving plate. Top sauce with one chicken breast; top chicken with spoonful of sauce. Serve with steamed vegetables and remaining sauce. Garnish, if desired.

Makes 8 servings

Step 4. Ground pecans.

Step 9. Stirring drippings into yogurt mixture.

Curried Chicken Rolls

1 medium onion
1 tablespoon butter or margarine
¾ cup hot cooked rice
¼ cup raisins
1 tablespoon chopped fresh
   parsley
1 teaspoon curry powder
1 teaspoon brown sugar
½ teaspoon poultry seasoning
   Pinch of garlic powder
2 whole chicken breasts, split,
   skinned and boned
   (pages 10–11)
½ teaspoon salt
⅛ teaspoon pepper
1 tablespoon vegetable oil
½ cup dry white wine
1 teaspoon instant chicken
   bouillon granules
   Apple quarters, orange slices
   and parsley sprigs for garnish

1. To prepare onion, peel skin from onion; cut in half through the root. Reserve one half for another use. Place other half, cut side down, on cutting board. To coarsely chop onion, hold knife horizontally. Make cuts parallel to board, almost to root end. Next, make vertical, lengthwise cuts, then slice across cuts to root end. (The closer the cuts are spaced, the finer the onion is chopped.).

2. Melt butter in large skillet over medium heat until foamy. Add onion; cook and stir about 3 minutes or until onion is soft. Remove from heat.

3. Stir rice, raisins, parsley, curry, brown sugar, poultry seasoning and garlic powder into skillet; mix well and set aside.

4. Flatten chicken breasts to ⅜-inch thickness (technique on pages 7–8); sprinkle with salt and pepper.

5. Divide rice mixture evenly between chicken breasts; spread to within 1 inch of edges.

6. Roll up each chicken breast from short end, jelly-roll fashion; secure with wooden toothpicks, making sure filling is entirely enclosed.

7. Heat oil in large skillet over medium heat; add chicken rolls to skillet in single layer. Cook 15 minutes or until rolls are brown on all sides. Add wine and bouillon to skillet; carefully stir until granules are dissolved. Cover; simmer 30 minutes or until chicken is tender. Garnish, if desired.

Makes 4 servings

Serving Suggestion: Additional rice stuffing may be prepared and served alongside the chicken rolls. Bake in covered casserole at 350°F until heated through.

Step 1. Chopping onion.

Step 5. Spreading rice mixture on chicken breasts.

Step 6. Rolling up filled chicken breast.

Sautéed Chicken Breasts in Cream Sauce

2 to 3 quarts water
2 whole chicken breasts, split, skinned and boned (pages 10–11)
1 medium onion
2 tablespoons margarine
1½ cups thinly sliced mushrooms
1 cup thinly sliced celery
½ teaspoon pepper
½ teaspoon dried basil leaves, crushed
¼ teaspoon dried chervil leaves, crushed
⅛ teaspoon dried thyme leaves, crushed
⅓ to ¾ cup dry white wine or sherry, divided
2½ cups (8 ounces) corkscrew pasta, uncooked
1 package (8 ounces) cream cheese
¼ cup milk
Chopped fresh parsley for garnish

1. Bring water to a boil in large saucepan or Dutch oven.

2. Meanwhile, cut chicken into thin strips on cutting board.

3. Chop half of onion (technique on page 32).

4. Melt margarine in large skillet over medium heat until foamy. Add chicken strips, onion, mushrooms, celery, pepper, basil, chervil and thyme. Cook 5 minutes or until chicken is tender, stirring occasionally. Set aside; keep warm.

5. Add 2 tablespoons wine; reduce heat and simmer 5 minutes.

6. When water boils, stir in pasta. Follow package directions for cooking time.

7. Meanwhile, to cube cream cheese, cut cheese crosswise, then lengthwise, into ½-inch cubes on cutting board.

8. When pasta is cooked, rinse and drain in colander in sink.

9. Combine cream cheese and milk in same saucepan; stir over low heat until smooth.

10. Blend in enough remaining wine to make sauce of pouring consistency.

11. Place pasta on serving platter. Top with chicken-vegetable mixture; pour cream sauce over chicken and pasta. Garnish, if desired.

Makes 4 to 6 servings

Step 2. Cutting chicken into thin strips.

Step 7. Cubed cream cheese.

Step 8. Rinsing and draining pasta.

Apricot Chicken Oriental

Nonstick cooking spray
16 dried apricots
2 tablespoons butter or margarine
2 whole chicken breasts, split, skinned and boned (pages 10–11)
1 jar (10 ounces) apricot preserves
3½ cups water, divided
½ cup soy sauce
1 can (8 ounces) sliced water chestnuts, drained and liquid reserved
1 teaspoon ground ginger
1 teaspoon garlic powder
¼ teaspoon salt
1 cup long-grain rice
1 red or green bell pepper
3 ribs celery, diagonally sliced
2 cups sliced mushrooms
1 bunch green onions, sliced
1 package (6 ounces) frozen pea pods
Bean sprouts for garnish

1. To chop apricots, spray blade of chef's knife with nonstick cooking spray. Arrange apricots in single layer on cutting board; chop apricots, spraying knife blade with nonstick cooking spray as needed to prevent sticking. Reserve ¼ cup apricots for rice mixture.

2. Melt butter in large skillet over medium heat until foamy. Add chicken to skillet in single layer; cook 10 minutes or until chicken is browned, turning once.

3. Stir in apricots, preserves, 1 cup water, soy sauce, liquid from water chestnuts, ginger and garlic powder. Simmer 25 minutes or until chicken is tender.

4. Meanwhile, combine remaining 2½ cups water, reserved ¼ cup apricots and salt in medium saucepan. Bring to a boil; stir in rice. Cover; reduce heat and simmer 20 minutes. Remove from heat; let stand 5 minutes.

5. Cut bell pepper in half lengthwise on cutting board; remove stem, seeds and membrane. Slice pepper lengthwise into strips on cutting board.

6. Add water chestnuts, bell pepper, celery, mushrooms, green onions and pea pods to skillet with chicken; cook and stir 5 minutes or until vegetables are heated through.

7. Place equal amounts of rice mixture on each serving plate. Arrange chicken and vegetables over rice. Garnish, if desired.

Makes 4 servings

Step 1. Chopping apricots.

Step 4. Stirring in rice.

Step 5. Removing membranes from pepper.

Chicken in Lemon Sauce

¹/₄ cup butter or margarine
4 whole chicken breasts, split,
   skinned and boned
   (pages 10–11)
1 lemon
2 tablespoons dry white wine
¹/₄ teaspoon salt
¹/₈ teaspoon white pepper
1 cup heavy cream
¹/₃ cup grated Parmesan cheese
1 cup sliced mushrooms
   Red grapes and grated lemon
   peel for garnish

1. Melt butter in large skillet over medium heat until foamy. Add chicken to skillet in single layer. Cook 10 minutes or until chicken is brown and no longer pink in center, turning once.

2. Remove chicken to broilerproof baking dish; set aside.

3. Drain drippings from skillet.

4. To prepare lemon, finely grate colored portion of peel to measure ¹/₂ teaspoon using bell grater or hand-held grater. Grate additional peel for garnish; set aside.

5. To juice lemon, cut lemon in half on cutting board; with tip of knife, remove visible seeds. Using citrus reamer, squeeze 2 tablespoons juice from lemon into small glass or dish; remove any remaining seeds from juice.

6. Add lemon peel, lemon juice and wine to skillet; cook and stir over medium heat 1 minute. Stir in salt and white pepper.

7. Gradually pour cream into skillet, stirring constantly. Simmer over medium-low heat until hot; *do not boil.*

8. Pour cream sauce over chicken; sprinkle with cheese and mushrooms.

9. Broil chicken about 6 inches from heat source until lightly browned. Arrange chicken breasts and sauce on serving platter. Garnish, if desired. *Makes 8 servings*

Step 4. Grating lemon peel.

Step 5. Removing seeds from lemon.

Step 7. Stirring cream into juice mixture.

Chicken with Fruit and Mixed Mustards

½ cup Dijon-style mustard
½ cup Bavarian or other German
    mustard
1 tablespoon Chinese mustard
⅓ cup honey
⅓ cup light cream
2 whole chicken breasts, split,
    skinned and boned
    (pages 10–11)
½ teaspoon salt
¼ teaspoon pepper
2 tablespoons butter
1 honeydew melon
1 cantaloupe
4 kiwifruit, peeled and sliced
    (page 90)
¼ cup mayonnaise
    Mint sprigs for garnish

1. Combine mustards, honey and cream in medium bowl. Spoon half of the mustard sauce into large glass bowl. Reserve remainder in medium bowl.

2. Sprinkle chicken with salt and pepper; add to large glass bowl with mustard sauce, turning to coat with sauce. Cover; marinate in refrigerator 30 minutes.

3. Heat butter in large skillet over medium heat until foamy. Remove chicken from mustard sauce marinade, shaking off excess. Add to skillet in single layer. Cook 10 minutes or until chicken is brown and no longer pink in center, turning once.

4. Remove chicken to cutting board. Discard mustard sauce marinade. Cut chicken across grain into thin slices; set aside.

5. To prepare melon balls, cut melons crosswise in half on cutting board. Remove seeds with spoon; discard. Make melon balls by scooping out equal amounts of melon flesh from each melon to total 2 cups using melon baller or half-teaspoon measuring spoon.

6. Arrange chicken, melon balls and kiwifruit on serving platter; set aside.

7. Place reserved mustard sauce in small saucepan. Whisk in mayonnaise. Heat thoroughly over medium heat.

8. Drizzle some mustard sauce over chicken. Garnish, if desired. Pass remaining sauce.

Makes 4 servings

Step 2. Coating chicken with mustard sauce marinade.

Step 4. Cutting chicken into thin slices.

Step 5. Scooping out melon balls.

Pollo alla Firènze

2 cups *plus* 2 tablespoons dry sherry, divided
3 whole chicken breasts, split and boned (pages 10–11)
2 cloves garlic
3 tablespoons olive oil
3 cups fresh spinach leaves, shredded
2 cups coarsely chopped mushrooms
1 cup grated carrots
⅓ cup sliced green onions
Salt and pepper to taste
1½ cups prepared Italian salad dressing
1 cup Italian seasoned dry bread crumbs
⅓ cup grated Romano cheese
Steamed fresh asparagus
Parsley sprigs and carrot strips for garnish

1. Pour 2 cups sherry into large, shallow dish. Add chicken, turning to coat. Cover; marinate in refrigerator 3 hours.

2. Chop garlic until minced (technique on page 30). Heat oil in large skillet over medium heat. Add garlic, spinach, mushrooms, grated carrots, green onions, salt, pepper and remaining 2 tablespoons sherry. Cook and stir 3 to 5 minutes or until spinach is completely wilted; cool spinach mixture.

3. Place dressing in another shallow dish; set aside. Combine bread crumbs with Romano cheese in shallow dish; set aside. Preheat oven to 375°F.

4. Remove chicken from marinade; discard marinade. Slice a pocket into side of each chicken breast where breasts were originally attached.

5. Fill pockets in chicken with spinach mixture.

6. Secure pockets with wooden toothpicks to enclose mixture.

7. Coat each filled chicken breast with dressing, shaking off excess. Place each chicken breast in bread crumb mixture; spoon bread crumb mixture over chicken to coat.

8. Place chicken in single layer in greased 13 × 9-inch baking pan. Drizzle with remaining dressing. Cover; bake 15 minutes. Uncover; bake 10 minutes or until chicken is tender. Serve with asparagus. Garnish, if desired. *Makes 6 servings*

Step 4. Slicing pocket into chicken breast.

Step 5. Filling pocket with spinach mixture.

Step 6. Enclosing filling with toothpicks.

Chicken Breasts Sautéed with Sun-Dried Tomatoes

Nonstick cooking spray
8 to 10 pieces sun-dried tomatoes
1 egg, beaten
1 container (15 ounces) Polly-O® ricotta cheese
1 package (4 ounces) Polly-O® shredded mozzarella cheese (1 cup)
1/3 cup Polly-O® grated Parmesan or Romano cheese
2 tablespoons chopped fresh parsley
1/2 teaspoon garlic powder
1/4 teaspoon pepper
4 whole chicken breasts, split, skinned and boned (pages 10–11)
2 tablespoons pine nuts
2 tablespoons currants
1/3 cup butter
2/3 cup sliced shallots
1 cup chicken broth
1/2 cup dry white wine
Sliced plum tomatoes, fresh thyme sprigs and additional pine nuts for garnish

1. To chop tomatoes, spray blade of chef's knife with nonstick cooking spray. Arrange tomatoes in single layer on cutting board; chop enough tomatoes to measure 1/3 cup, spraying knife blade with nonstick cooking spray as needed to prevent sticking. Slice remaining tomatoes into strips; reserve and set aside.

2. Combine chopped tomatoes, egg, cheeses, parsley, garlic powder and pepper in medium bowl. Stir to mix well; set aside.

3. Flatten chicken breasts to 1/4-inch thickness (technique on page 7–8); set aside.

4. Divide cheese mixture evenly between chicken breasts; spread to within 1 inch of edges. Sprinkle pine nuts and currants over cheese mixture.

5. Roll up chicken from short end, jelly-roll fashion; enclose filling and secure with wooden toothpicks.

6. Melt butter in large skillet over medium-high heat until foamy. Add chicken to skillet; cook until golden on all sides. Remove chicken; set aside.

7. Add shallots and reserved tomato strips to drippings in skillet; cook over low heat 2 minutes. Add broth and wine; cook 3 minutes.

8. Return chicken to skillet. Cover; simmer 15 to 20 minutes or until tender, turning once and basting often with sauce. Place chicken on platter; pour sauce over chicken. Garnish, if desired.

Makes 8 servings

Step 1. Chopping tomatoes.

Step 5. Rolling up filled chicken breast.

Curried Chicken Calcutta

¼ cup all-purpose flour
½ teaspoon curry powder
½ teaspoon ground cinnamon
½ teaspoon ground ginger
¼ teaspoon garlic powder
2 whole chicken breasts, split,
skinned and boned
(pages 10–11)
¼ cup vegetable oil
1 lime
1 cup plain yogurt
Cooked julienned carrots
Quartered lime slices and mint
sprigs for garnish

1. Combine flour, curry, cinnamon, ginger and garlic powder in shallow dish.

2. Coat chicken, one piece at a time, in flour mixture, shaking off excess.

3. Heat oil in large skillet over medium heat. Add chicken to skillet in single layer; cook until chicken is brown on both sides. Cover; reduce heat to low and cook 15 minutes or until chicken is tender and no longer pink in center.

4. Remove chicken to paper-towel-lined baking sheets, using tongs or slotted spoon; keep warm in preheated 200°F oven.

5. To prepare lime, finely grate colored portion of peel using bell grater or hand-held grater; set aside. To juice lime, cut lime in half on cutting board; with tip of knife, remove any visible seeds.

6. Using citrus reamer or squeezing tightly with hand, squeeze juice from lime into small saucepan; remove any remaining seeds from saucepan.

7. Combine yogurt with lime juice in saucepan. Cook over low heat, stirring constantly, until warm.

8. Arrange chicken on serving platter. Spoon about half of the yogurt sauce over chicken; sprinkle with grated lime peel. Pass remaining yogurt sauce. Serve with carrots. Garnish, if desired.   *Makes 4 servings*

Step 4. Transferring chicken to prepared baking sheets.

Step 5. Grating lime peel.

Step 6. Squeezing juice from lime.

Cranberry Smothered Chicken

3 cloves garlic
½ cup all-purpose flour
   Salt and white pepper to taste
3 whole chicken breasts, split and
   skinned (pages 10–11)
¼ cup vegetable oil
½ cup chicken broth
2 medium green bell peppers
3 medium onions
2 tablespoons butter or
   margarine
10 large mushrooms, sliced
½ cup raspberry or balsamic
   vinegar
1 can (16 ounces) whole berry
   cranberry sauce
1 cup orange juice
1 tablespoon cornstarch
1 tablespoon Worcestershire
   sauce
   Water
   Hot cooked rice and steamed
   fresh asparagus
   Orange slices and parsley
   sprigs for garnish

1. To prepare garlic, trim ends of garlic cloves. Slightly crush garlic under flat side of knife blade; peel away skins. Arrange garlic together in small pile; chop until minced.

2. Combine flour, salt and white pepper in large resealable plastic bag.

3. Add chicken to bag; shake to coat completely with flour mixture.

4. Heat oil in large skillet over medium-high heat. Add garlic; cook until soft. Add chicken; cook until chicken is browned on both sides. Drain drippings from skillet. Add chicken broth; bring to a boil over high heat. Reduce heat to low. Cover; simmer 30 minutes.

5. To prepare bell peppers, with paring knife, make circular cuts around tops of peppers. Pull stems from peppers to remove stems, seeds and membranes. Rinse out peppers under running water to remove any excess seeds; drain well. Slice peppers lengthwise in half on cutting board; remove any excess membrane. Thinly slice each half lengthwise into thin strips.

continued on page 80

Step 1. Crushing garlic.

Step 3. Coating chicken with flour mixture.

Step 5. Slicing pepper into thin strips.

Cranberry Smothered Chicken, continued

6. To prepare onions, peel skins from onions; cut in half through the roots. Place, cut sides down, on cutting board. To coarsely chop onions, hold knife horizontally. Make cuts parallel to board, almost to root ends. Next, make vertical, lengthwise cuts, then slice across cuts to root ends. (The closer the cuts are spaced, the finer the onions are chopped.)

7. Melt butter in another large skillet over medium-high heat. Cook and stir peppers, onions and mushrooms in hot butter until vegetables are softened. Stir in vinegar, cranberry sauce and orange juice. Reduce heat to medium. Cook and stir about 5 minutes until cranberry sauce melts and mixture is heated through.

8. Mix cornstarch and Worcestershire sauce with enough water to make a smooth paste; add to sauce and vegetables in skillet. Stir gently over low heat until thickened. Season with salt and white pepper.

9. Arrange chicken, rice and asparagus on individual serving plates. Pour sauce over chicken. Garnish, if desired.

Makes 6 servings

Step 6. Chopping onions.

Step 8. Adding cornstarch mixture.

Greek-Style Chicken in Phyllo

3 whole chicken breasts, split, skinned and boned (pages 10–11)
2 tablespoons vegetable oil
1 package (10 ounces) frozen chopped spinach
1 large onion
1 clove garlic
¼ cup butter
1 can (4 ounces) sliced mushrooms, drained
2 tablespoons chopped fresh parsley
1½ tablespoons finely chopped fresh dill weed
1½ tablespoons all-purpose flour
⅓ cup vermouth
1 cup (8 ounces) Polly-O® ricotta cheese, well drained
Salt and pepper to taste
½ cup melted butter
12 sheets phyllo dough*
Seasoned dry bread crumbs
Sliced tomatoes sprinkled with fresh oregano

*Cover with damp kitchen towel to prevent dough from drying out.

1. Place chicken breasts between two pieces of plastic wrap. Pound with flat side of meat mallet to ¼-inch thickness (technique on pages 7–8); set aside.

2. Heat oil in large skillet over medium heat. Add chicken to skillet in single layer. Cook until chicken is lightly browned. Remove chicken to paper towels to drain; set aside. Wipe out skillet.

3. Cook spinach according to package directions. Drain. To remove excess liquid from spinach, place in bottom of pie plate. Place another pie plate on top. Over sink, squeeze plates together and tilt slightly to press excess liquid from spinach; set aside.

4. To prepare onion, peel skin from onion; cut in half through the root. Place, cut side down, on cutting board. To coarsely chop onion, hold knife horizontally. Make cuts parallel to board, almost to root end. Next, make vertical, lengthwise cuts, then slice across cuts to root end. (The closer the cuts are spaced, the finer the onion is chopped.)

5. To prepare garlic, trim ends of clove. Slightly crush clove under flat side of knife blade. Peel away skin. Chop garlic until minced; set aside.

continued on page 82

Step 3. Squeezing excess liquid from spinach.

Step 4. Chopping onion.

Step 5. Crushing garlic.

Greek-Style Chicken in Phyllo, continued

6. Melt ¼ cup butter in same skillet over medium heat. Add onion; cook and stir until golden. Add spinach, garlic, mushrooms, parsley and dill; cook and stir 2 minutes.

7. Stir in flour, mixing well. Gradually stir in vermouth; cook and stir until thickened. Stir in ricotta cheese, salt and pepper; remove spinach mixture from heat and set aside.

8. Preheat oven to 350°F.

9. Brush small amount of ½ cup melted butter onto 1 phyllo sheet; sprinkle with bread crumbs. Cover with second phyllo sheet; brush with butter. Place chicken breast in center of top phyllo sheet; spoon ⅙ of spinach mixture on top.

10. Fold long edges of phyllo sheets over chicken and spinach mixture. Fold short edges of phyllo over chicken and spinach mixture so that they overlap; roll bundle to enclose filling. Repeat with remaining phyllo sheets, butter, bread crumbs, chicken breasts and spinach mixture.

11. Place bundles in single layer, seam sides down, in greased baking pan. Brush tops with butter. Bake 45 minutes or until brown and slightly puffed. Serve with tomatoes.

Makes 6 servings

Step 9. Positioning chicken in phyllo.

Step 10. Folding phyllo over chicken.

Chicken Avocado Melt

2 tablespoons cornstarch
1 teaspoon ground cumin
1 teaspoon garlic salt
1 egg
1 tablespoon water
⅓ cup yellow cornmeal
2 whole chicken breasts, split, skinned and boned (pages 10–11)
3 tablespoons vegetable oil
1 firm ripe avocado
1½ cups (6 ounces) shredded Monterey Jack cheese
½ cup sour cream
¼ cup sliced green onion tops
4 green onion brushes for garnish (page 35)
¼ cup chopped red bell pepper (page 40)
Steamed crinkle-cut carrots

1. Preheat oven to 325°F. Combine cornstarch, cumin and garlic salt in shallow dish; set aside. Beat egg with water in shallow dish; set aside. Place cornmeal in shallow dish; set aside.

2. Flatten chicken breasts to ¼-inch thickness (technique on pages 7–8).

3. Coat chicken in cornstarch mixture, shaking off excess. Dip chicken into egg mixture, then roll in cornmeal, shaking off excess.

4. Heat oil in large skillet over medium-high heat. Add chicken to skillet in single layer; cook 4 minutes, turning once.

5. Remove chicken to shallow baking dish; set aside.

6. Remove pit from avocado (technique on page 54); cut avocado halves lengthwise in half on cutting board. From stem end, carefully peel skin away from each avocado quarter.

7. Cut avocado quarters lengthwise into slices; set aside.

8. Arrange avocado slices over chicken in dish; sprinkle with cheese.

9. Bake chicken 15 minutes or until chicken is tender and cheese is melted. Transfer chicken to serving platter. Top each serving with a dollop of sour cream; sprinkle with sliced green onion tops and red pepper. Serve with carrots. Garnish, if desired.

Makes 4 servings

Step 3. Coating chicken in cornstarch mixture.

Step 6. Peeling skin from avocado quarters.

Step 7. Cutting avocado into slices.

Coconut Chicken with Fresh Chutney

1 can (15 ounces) cream of
  coconut, divided
2 tablespoons soy sauce
2 whole chicken breasts, split
  (pages 10–11) or 8 chicken
  thighs
½ lemon
1 small piece fresh ginger
  (1×¾ inch)
1 clove garlic
3 cups chopped nectarines or
  apples
½ cup raisins
⅓ cup packed light brown sugar
¼ cup cider vinegar
½ teaspoon curry powder
¼ cup flaked coconut

1. To prepare coconut marinade, combine ¾ cup cream of coconut and soy sauce in small bowl.

2. Arrange chicken in single layer in 12×7-inch glass baking dish. Pour coconut marinade over chicken, turning chicken to coat with coconut marinade. Cover; marinate in refrigerator overnight.

3. Meanwhile, to prepare chutney mixture, with tip of knife, remove any visible seeds from lemon half.

4. Chop lemon to measure ¼ cup; set aside.

5. Peel ginger; chop until minced.

6. To prepare garlic, trim ends of clove on cutting board. Slightly crush garlic under flat side of knife blade; peel away skin. Chop garlic until minced.

7. Combine lemon, ginger, garlic, nectarines, raisins, brown sugar, vinegar and curry in medium saucepan; mix well. Bring to a boil; boil 2 minutes, stirring occasionally. Cool chutney mixture.

8. Add flaked coconut and remaining cream of coconut; mix well. Cover chutney mixture; refrigerate overnight to allow flavors to blend.

9. Preheat oven to 350°F. Bake chicken in dish with coconut marinade 45 minutes to 1 hour or until chicken is tender, basting frequently with coconut marinade.

10. Place chicken on individual serving plates. Spoon equal amounts of the chutney mixture alongside chicken. Garnish as desired.

Makes 4 servings

Step 3. Removing seeds from lemon half.

Step 4. Chopping lemon.

Step 6. Minced garlic.

Chicken with Cucumbers and Dill

2 whole chicken breasts, split, skinned and boned (pages 10–11)
1 teaspoon salt, divided
3/4 teaspoon pepper, divided
4 tablespoons butter, divided
2 cucumbers
1/2 teaspoon dried dill weed, crushed
1/4 cup lemon juice
Quartered lemon slices and dill sprigs for garnish

1. Sprinkle chicken breasts with 1/2 teaspoon salt and 1/2 teaspoon pepper.

2. Melt 2 tablespoons butter in large skillet over medium heat until foamy. Add chicken to skillet in single layer. Cook 10 minutes or until chicken is no longer pink in center, turning once.

3. Remove chicken to paper-towel-lined baking sheets, using tongs or slotted spoon; keep warm in preheated 200°F oven. Drain drippings from skillet; reserve.

4. To prepare cucumbers, peel skins from cucumbers using vegetable peeler. Cut peeled cucumbers in half lengthwise on cutting board; remove seeds. Cut halves crosswise into 1/4-inch slices.

5. Melt remaining 2 tablespoons butter in same skillet until foamy. Add cucumbers; stir to coat with butter. Sprinkle remaining 1/2 teaspoon salt and 1/4 teaspoon pepper over cucumbers; cook 2 minutes. Stir in dill. Push cucumbers to side of skillet.

6. Return chicken and drippings to skillet. Cook 2 minutes or until chicken is heated through.

7. Place chicken on serving platter; arrange cucumbers around chicken.

8. Cook drippings in skillet over medium heat until light brown. Pour lemon juice and drippings over chicken. Garnish, if desired.

Makes 4 servings

Step 2. Cooking chicken.

Step 4. Peeling cucumber.

Roast Chicken & Kiwi with Raspberry Glaze

2 (3½- to 4-pound) frying
  chickens, cut into halves
  (page 9)
1 teaspoon salt
¼ teaspoon pepper
½ cup butter, melted
  Raspberry Glaze
  (recipe follows)
2 kiwifruit

1. Preheat oven to 400°F. Sprinkle chicken halves with salt and pepper.

2. Place chicken halves, skin sides up, in single layer in large shallow baking pan. Brush chicken with butter.

3. Roast chicken, basting frequently with butter, 45 minutes or until chicken is tender.

4. Meanwhile, prepare Raspberry Glaze.

5. To prepare kiwifruit, remove peel from kiwifruit with vegetable peeler or paring knife.

6. Cut kiwifruit into thin slices; set aside.

7. When chicken is done, spoon off drippings from baking pan.

8. Spoon Raspberry Glaze over chicken; top with kiwifruit slices.

9. Bake chicken 3 minutes or until kiwifruit and chicken are well glazed, spooning glaze frequently from bottom of pan over chicken and kiwifruit. *Makes 4 servings*

Step 5. Peeling kiwifruit.

Step 6. Slicing peeled kiwifruit.

Step 7. Spooning off drippings.

Raspberry Glaze

1 cup seedless raspberry preserves
½ cup white port wine
  Grated peel of 1 lemon (page 68)

Combine preserves, wine and lemon peel in small saucepan; cook over low heat 5 minutes or until thickened slightly.

Makes about 1 cup

Stuffed Chicken with Apple Glaze

1 (3½- to 4-pound) whole frying chicken
½ teaspoon salt
¼ teaspoon pepper
2 tablespoons vegetable oil
1 package (6 ounces) chicken-flavored stuffing mix *plus* ingredients to prepare mix
1 large apple
½ teaspoon grated lemon peel (page 68)
¼ cup chopped walnuts
¼ cup raisins
¼ cup thinly sliced celery
½ cup apple jelly
1 tablespoon lemon juice
½ teaspoon ground cinnamon
Celery leaves and lemon peel twists for garnish

1. Preheat oven to 350°F.

2. Rinse chicken under cold running water; pat dry with paper towels. Sprinkle inside of chicken with salt and pepper; rub outside with oil.

3. Prepare stuffing mix according to package directions in large bowl.

4. To prepare apple, cut lengthwise into quarters on cutting board; remove stem, core and seeds with paring knife. Chop apple quarters into ½-inch pieces.

5. Add apple, lemon peel, walnuts, raisins and celery to prepared stuffing; mix thoroughly.

6. Stuff body cavity loosely with stuffing.

7. Place chicken in shallow baking pan. Cover loosely with foil; roast chicken 1 hour.

8. Combine jelly, lemon juice and cinnamon in small saucepan. Simmer over low heat 3 minutes, stirring often, until jelly dissolves and mixture is well blended.

9. Remove foil from chicken; brush with jelly glaze.

10. Roast chicken, uncovered, brushing frequently with jelly glaze, 30 minutes or until meat thermometer inserted into thickest part of thigh, not touching bone, registers 185°F. Let chicken stand 15 minutes before carving. Garnish, if desired. *Makes 4 servings*

Step 4. Removing stem, core and seeds from apple.

Step 6. Stuffing chicken.

Step 9. Brushing chicken with jelly glaze.

INDEX